The Character of the Christian

TIM CHALLIES

CRUCIFORM PRESS | DECEMBER 2017

CruciformPress
@CHALLIES

CruciformPress.com | info@CruciformPress.com

AUTHOR

Tim Challies is a Christian, a husband to Aileen, and a father to three children aged 11 to 17. He is a co-founder of Cruciform Press and has written several books, including *Visual Theology*, *Do More Better*, and *Sexual Detox*. He worships and serves as a pastor at Grace Fellowship Church in Toronto, Ontario and writes daily at www.challies.com.

 *We all know the feeling: every week, every month, every year it just seems that life keeps moving faster and faster. So we've taken our trademark length—books of about 100 pages—and added a set of resources that will make for even a quicker read. Cruciform Quick: a new line of booklets in the range of 40 to 60 pages each.*

THE CHARACTER OF THE CHRISTIAN

Print / PDF ISBN: 978-1-941114-36-0
Mobipocket ISBN: 978-1-941114-37-7
ePub ISBN: 978-1-941114-38-4

Table of Contents

Remarkably Unremarkable

Every true Christian wants to grow in spiritual maturity. We all want to put on the new self and put off the old, throwing away patterns of sin and replacing them with patterns of holiness. Ultimately, we want to become like Christ, to think how he thought and behave how he behaved. We do well to aspire to the highest standard of holiness and godliness.

The Bible holds out one group of people who are to serve as models of Christian maturity: elders (sometimes referred to as pastors or overseers). Elders are qualified for their office primarily on the basis of their character. While the Bible provides one quality related to skill, all of the other qualifications are related to character. Yet while these traits are required of elders, they are not exclusive to elders.

D.A. Carson has pointed out that the list of qualifications for elders is "remarkable for being unremarkable."[1] Why? Because these traits are repeated elsewhere as qualities that ought to characterize all believers. Carson says, "The criteria mentioned are demanded of all Christians everywhere. Which is another way of saying, elders are first of all to be exemplars of the Christian graces that are presupposed as mandated on all Christians." Every church is meant to be full of men and women who display these traits.

There is an important application for every Christian: if you want to grow in holiness, one great way to begin is by knowing and imitating the character qualifications of elders. That is exactly the purpose of this booklet. It examines the character of a Christian by going deep into the character qualifications of elders. I hope to answer questions like these: In what ways do the qualifications of an elder and the calling of all Christians overlap? Very practically, what do these qualities look like in the life of the believer? How can I know if I am displaying these qualities? And how can I best pray for them in my own life?

As we go, we will consider how to spur one another on to good works, growing in Christlikeness and abounding in love. I hope you will follow along with a prayerful spirit as we learn together how to exemplify the highest Christian virtues. Here is a sneak peek of the ground we will be covering:

- Above Reproach
- A One-Woman Man (or A One-Man Woman)
- Disciplined
- Hospitable
- Gentle
- Temperate
- Generous
- Family Leaders
- Mature and Humble
- Respected by Outsiders [2]

HOW TO USE THIS BOOKLET

There are many ways to use this booklet, and you are free to use it however it suits you. But I recommend reading at a slow pace and allowing each chapter to nudge you toward greater self-examination and prayer. At the end of each chapter, you will find self-reflection questions and prayers asking God to grant you the graces we have discussed. I believe these will have as much enduring value as the words that precede them.

CHAPTER 1

Above Reproach

The purpose of this booklet is to explore how the character qualifications of elders are actually God's calling on all Christians. While elders are meant to exemplify these traits, all Christians are to follow their example by displaying them. I want us to consider whether we actually display these traits and learn together how we can pray to have them in greater measure.

We begin with the qualification of "above reproach." This is found in 1 Timothy 3:2 ("Therefore an overseer must be above reproach") and twice in Titus 1:6-7. Whatever it means to be above reproach, it is clearly not only expected of church leaders. Paul teaches that the great hope and comfort of every Christian is that God himself will one day "present you holy and blameless and above reproach before him" (Colossians 1:22). An above-reproach lifestyle is for every Christian. John MacArthur points out that the reason this qualification is necessary at the pastoral level is because pastors are to be the example that others follow. And if being above reproach "is part of that example, then guess what is required of you? The same [trait]."[3]

What does it mean to be "above reproach"? The Greek term denotes a kind of innocence in the eyes of the law. It indicates a lifestyle against which no one can make any legitimate charges. Others may bring accusations, but your blameless conduct will eventually acquit you. Your life is so consistent that your behavior sets an example, your reputation demands honor, and your practice adorns the gospel by matching what you preach.

Naturally, before we can live above reproach, we must know exactly what "above reproach" entails. In his book *Biblical Eldership*, Alexander Strauch explains, "What is meant by 'above reproach' is defined by the character qualities that follow the term."[4] Thus, being "above reproach" is expressed through those other qualities in 1 Timothy 3, Titus 1, and 1 Peter 5.

Being above reproach in your marriage means you are "the husband of one wife." Being above reproach in your thought life means you are "sober-minded." Being above reproach in your actions means you are "self-controlled." As we can see, this is a summary attribute, indicating that the above-reproach Christian is one who upholds all of the character traits that God commends. Of course, being above reproach does not mean being perfect. But it does mean living in the light, confessing our sins, and turning from them because our standard is perfection (Matthew 5:48).

The best way to pursue an above-reproach lifestyle is through God's means of grace—reading the Bible and deliberately applying it, praying privately and with your family, attending your church's worship services faithfully, participating in the ordinances of baptism and Lord's Supper, and so on. These are the channels through which God sends his sanctifying grace. Apart from them, you cannot expect to attain or maintain an above-reproach life.

SELF-EVALUATION

The most thorough evaluation of your life will come in the following chapters, as we examine the more precise character qualifications that are summarized by this one. But in the meantime, these questions will help you consider whether you are living in a manner that is above reproach.

- *Are there any ongoing sins in your life that would bring shame to you, your family, and your local church if they were made public? Are there any parts of your life that you deliberately hide from others?*

- *Do you know what sins you are especially prone to commit? Do you have measures in your life to guard against the temptation to these sins?*

- *Are you taking advantage of God's means of grace? Are you regularly attending church and participating in the life of the church? Do you have times of private and family worship?*

- *Do you think your life right now is pleasing to God? When it is not, are you quick to seek the forgiveness of both God and man? Do you display repentance by making significant changes?*

- *Imagine that your close friends or people in your church heard charges against your character. Would their reaction be, "That's not possible," or "I knew it"? What does this response say about you?*

PRAYER POINTS

As we begin considering Christian character, we need to acknowledge that attaining this is possible only through God's grace. God works in his children that which is pleasing in his sight (Hebrews 13:20–21). He finishes the good work he started (Philippians 1:6). So as we aim to be above reproach, we must begin with fear and trembling, humbly depending upon the one who enables us to will and work for his good pleasure (Philippians 2:12-13). This is why we must pray to gain these qualities, to uphold them, and to grow in them. To that end, here are some ways you may pray:

- *I pray that I would joyfully and obediently do all things without grumbling or disputing, that I may be blameless and innocent, your child without blemish in the midst of a crooked and twisted generation, among whom I shine as a light in the world (Philippians 2:14–15).*

- *I pray that your Holy Spirit would help me identify sin in my life wherever it exists and put it to death.*

- *I pray that my pursuit of holiness would be firmly rooted in the gospel.*

- *I pray that I would walk in blamelessness before you and my neighbor. Make my conduct match my profession, so that my life does not display even a trace of hypocrisy.*

- *I pray that when I sin I would be quick to seek your forgiveness and the forgiveness of those I sinned against.*

- *I pray that if charges are ever brought against my character, I will be found innocent—blameless in your sight.*

CHAPTER 2

A One-Woman Man
(Or a One-Man Woman)

As we continue this extended look at the character of the Christian, we are exploring how the various character qualifications of elders are actually God's calling on all Christians. While elders are meant to exemplify these traits, all Christians are to follow their example by displaying them. I want us to consider whether we possess these traits, and learn together how we can pray to have them in greater measure.

Our topic in this chapter is a qualification Paul repeats in both 1 Timothy 3:2 and Titus 1:6. The ESV translates it as "the husband of one wife," a common rendering of the literal Greek: "a one-woman man." There are several ways we could interpret this qualification. Does it mean that a pastor must not be a polygamist? Does it mean that an elder must be married? Does it disqualify pastors who have been divorced and remarried? None of these quite get to the heart of the matter. John MacArthur says, "It's not concerning status, it is concerning character. It is not a matter of circumstance; it is a matter of his virtue. And the issue here is a man who is solely and only and totally devoted to the woman who is his wife. It is a question of his character. He is a one-woman man. Anything less is a disqualification."[5]

Similarly, Strauch reminds us that the home is the first litmus test of an above-reproach lifestyle. He writes,

> In both of Paul's qualification lists, he places the
> qualification "the husband of one wife" immediately

after "above reproach." So the first and foremost area in which an elder must be above reproach is in his marital and sexual life.... The phrase "the husband of one wife" is meant to be a positive statement that expresses faithful, monogamous marriage. In English we would say, "faithful and true to one woman" or "a one-woman man."[6]

Philip Ryken says that Paul "wants the leaders of the church to be living examples of biblical marriage: one man and one woman in a love covenant for life."[7]

The qualified elder models the sexual integrity that is expected of all Christians. This is true whether the Christian is married or single, male or female. Paul commands the whole congregation in Corinth to "flee from sexual immorality" and warns them of the especially destructive nature of sexual sin (1 Corinthians 6:18). Writing to the gathered church in Ephesus, Paul sets the standard so high as to demand, "Sexual immorality and all impurity or covetousness must not even be named among you, as is proper among saints" (Ephesians 5:3). Paul is clear: if you are "sexually immoral or impure," then you have "no inheritance in the kingdom of Christ and God" (Ephesians 5:5).

Of course, as with all of these qualifications, we will not exemplify them perfectly. That's why we must always come back to the gospel of Jesus Christ, returning to his forgiveness and depending on his power for future sanctification. Paul also says that even though some in the congregation had once been "sexually immoral," counted among those who had no inheritance in the kingdom of God, he goes on to say: "But you were washed, you were sanctified, you were justified in the name of the Lord Jesus Christ and by the Spirit of our God" (1 Corinthians 6:9-11). He reminds them that their sexual sin is related to the old man and its evil ways, not the new man and its righteous ways.

Still, we must take seriously the New Testament's undeniable call to sexual purity. It is a call to devotion—first to God and then to a God-given spouse. It is a call away from adultery, to be sure. But even further, it is a call away from a wandering heart, wandering eyes, and wandering hands. It is a call for purity and chastity, for exemplary character and conduct in marriage or singleness. It is a call for the married to pursue and enjoy sex with one another, and it is a call for the unmarried to willingly submit their sexuality to the purpose of their loving God.

SELF-EVALUATION

To strengthen your fight against sexual immorality and your fight for sexual purity, I encourage you to evaluate yourself in light of questions like these:

- *Are there any sexual sins you have committed that you need to confess? Are there any sins you have been hiding that you need to expose (Psalm 32:3–7)?*

- *Are there certain settings where you are especially prone to sexual failure? What precautions have you taken to avoid these settings? Are there radical actions that you still need to take (Matthew 5:27–30)?*

- *Does your marriage serve as an example of God's design and ideal for marriage? Are you faithful to your spouse in your thoughts, words, and actions? Do you regularly pursue sexual union with your spouse (1 Corinthians 7:3–5)?*

- *Do you indulge in entertainment that debases God's design and purpose for sexuality? Or do you willingly abstain from every form of evil and refuse to make light of it (1 Thessalonians 5:22; Ephesians 5:3)?*

PRAYER POINTS

We must pray to fight against the pull of sexual immorality. We must pray for the strength to pursue purity according to God's design. Let me encourage you to pray in these ways:

- *I pray, "Search me, O God, and know my heart! Try me and know my thoughts! And see if there be any grievous way in me, and lead me in the way everlasting!" (Psalm 139:23–24)?*

- *I pray that you would give me the desire and wisdom to guard my heart from all forms of sexual immorality. I pray that I would be quick to confess and turn from all known sexual sin. (Consider praying through Proverbs 6:23–35).*

- **For Men:** *I pray that I would regard older women as mothers and younger women as sisters, in all purity (1 Timothy 5:1–2).*

- **For Women:** *I pray that I would regard older men as fathers and younger men as brothers, in all purity (1 Timothy 5:1–2).*

- *I pray that you would purify my heart so that the sin of adultery—expressed even in lustful thoughts and glances—would lose all of its power over me (Matthew 5:27–30).*

- *I pray that I would not become despondent when I sin. Please let me take comfort in the knowledge that when I confess my sins, you are faithful and just to forgive my sins and cleanse me from all unrighteousness (1 John 1:9).*

CHAPTER 3

Disciplined

This chapter bundles together a set of three traits that are closely related to one another. 1 Timothy 3:2 (which is paralleled in Titus 1:8) says that elders must be "sober-minded, self-controlled, [and] respectable." What does it mean to be sober-minded? What does it mean to be self-controlled? And what does it mean to be respectable? We are grouping these words together because of their shared emphasis on a kind of self-mastery that leads to sound judgment.

"Sober-minded" is a word that relates primarily to the mind. The sober-minded man is clear-headed and watchful, free from excesses and wild fluctuations in thinking and ideas. This trait allows him to keep alert so he can protect himself and others from any kind of spiritual danger. He is not rash, but thoughtful.

Where "sober-minded" relates to the mind, "self-controlled" relates to actions or behavior. The self-controlled elder is free from excesses and wild fluctuations in his behavior. He willingly submits his emotions and passions to the control of the Holy Spirit and makes wise, thoughtful judgments. He shows restraint and moderation in all areas of life. Thabiti Anyabwile says those who exhibit this trait are "sensible, discreet, and wise."[8] They do not live for the moment, but consider the future consequences of their actions.

Those who are sober-minded and self-controlled are also "respectable." This word refers to an overall orderliness of life that draws respect from others. By their well-ordered lives and prudence, they demonstrate the ability to bring peaceful order to those around them. They know how to make wise decisions and live out the kind of practical wisdom described in the book of Proverbs. They are people for whom others have high esteem.

When we put these traits together, we see a person who has mastered his thinking and behavior so that he can make wise judgments. His own life is a showcase of such wisdom. Anyabwile aptly summarizes the importance of this trait:

> The ministry and the church are always being watched by people inside and outside, and the church's enemies continually look for opportunities to condemn it and slander it. Churches are greatly helped to withstand this onslaught when its leaders are respectable in their conduct and are men of sound judgment.[9]

Of course, God does not only call elders or prospective elders to be "sober-minded, self-controlled, and respectable"— he calls every Christian to pursue these traits. Let's start with sober-minded. In Romans 12:3, Paul writes, "For by the grace given to me I say to everyone among you not to think of himself more highly than he ought to think, but to think with sober judgment, each according to the measure of faith that God has assigned." Later, in 1 Thessalonians 5:6, he says, "So then let us not sleep, as others do, but let us keep awake and be sober."

When it comes to self-control, Solomon warns, "A man without self-control is like a city broken into and left without walls" (Proverbs 25:28). Paul includes self-control in the fruit of the Spirit and warns that those without self-control fall prey to Satan's temptations (Galatians 5:23; 1 Corinthians 7:5). He explicitly commands it of all believers in Titus 2:2-6. What Alexander Strauch says of elders is true of every believer: he must be "characterized by self-control and self-discipline in every aspect of life, particularly in his physical desires (Acts

24:25; 1 Corinthians 7:9, 9:25). An undisciplined man has little resistance to sexual lust, anger, slothfulness, a critical spirit, or other base desires. He is easy prey for the devil."[10]

As for respectability, Peter says, "in your hearts honor Christ the Lord as holy, always being prepared to make a defense to anyone who asks you for a reason for the hope that is in you; *yet do it with gentleness and respect,* having a good conscience, so that, when you are slandered, those who revile your good behavior in Christ may be put to shame" (1 Peter 3:15–16). Paul writes, "Pay to all what is owed to them: taxes to whom taxes are owed, revenue to whom revenue is owed, *respect to whom respect is owed,* honor to whom honor is owed" (Romans 13:7).

The Bible is clear that while these traits must be exemplified in elders, they are to be present in all believers. The character of the elder describes the character we should all pursue and exhibit.

SELF-EVALUATION

Would others say that you are "sober-minded, self-controlled, and respectable"? I encourage you to evaluate yourself in light of these questions:

- *When things do not go your way or when someone points out sin in your life, do you tend to respond with patient humility or with fits of anger? Would your spouse, children, or parents agree?*

- *Do you have any unrestrained or unhealthy habits in what you eat or drink or in your entertainment? Or are you joyfully submitted to the Holy Spirit in all of these things?*

- *Do you exhibit consistency and discipline in the spiritual (prayer, Bible reading, church involvement), relational (speech, purity, kindness), and bodily (exercise, diet, moderation) aspects of your life?*

- *Do you maintain a schedule? Do you generally bring your tasks to completion and do so with excellence?*

- *Are you confident in what you believe, or are you easily swayed by new books, new teachers, or new ideas? Do people seek your counsel when they are uncertain or facing a difficult decision?*

PRAYER POINTS

Apart from Christ, we can do nothing (John 15:5), so we need his strength if we are to grow in self-mastery. Let me encourage you to pray in these ways:

- *I pray that you would fill me with your Spirit so that self-control reigns in my heart and life (Galatians 5:23).*

- *I pray that you would help me put others first so that I do not think of myself more highly than I ought to think. Help me to think with appropriately sober judgment (Philippians 2:3; Romans 12:3).*

- *I pray that you would help me be slow to anger so that I have control over my temper (Proverbs 16:32).*

- *I pray that others would ask me about the hope within me because of my joyful, respectable life (1 Peter 3:14–17).*

CHAPTER 4

Hospitable

Our focus for this chapter is on what it means for an elder—and for every Christian—to be hospitable. We will also see why God elevates this trait to such high importance.

Paul tells Timothy that "an overseer must be ... hospitable" (1 Timothy 3:2) and echoes this in his letter to Titus (1:8). The Greek word for "hospitable" indicates a love for strangers. In a day when public inns were dirty, dangerous, and unsavory, Christians were expected to open their homes to traveling believers or itinerant preachers. They were to feed them and provide them with a safe place to sleep. *Hospitable* is naturally expanded to include other forms of hospitality, but it primarily indicates a willingness to invite others into your home for a short or extended stay.

Why is there such emphasis on this trait? Hospitality is a tangible, outward display of godly character. Strauch explains,

> Hospitality is a concrete expression of Christian love and family life. It is an important biblical virtue.... Giving oneself to the care of God's people means sharing one's life and home with others. An open home is a sign of an open heart and a loving, sacrificial, serving spirit. A lack of hospitality is a sure sign of selfish, lifeless, loveless Christianity.[11]

Opening our home is not only an act of Christian love itself, but it also enables more opportunities for Christian love. Hospitality allows us to deepen relationships, disciple others, and share the gospel. It creates a natural context for modeling marriage, parenting, and a host of Christian virtues.

While we are to teach others what the Bible says, we are also to demonstrate what it says. One of the best ways we can do that is by inviting people into our homes and into our lives.

Is it only elders who are called to share their lives and their resources by opening their homes? No, this call goes to all Christians. While the Old Testament places great emphasis on caring for and protecting the sojourner, this care for strangers is made even more explicit in the New Testament. Peter writes to all Christians when he says, "Show hospitality to one another without grumbling" (1 Peter 4:9). Paul tells the whole congregation in Rome that they must "seek to show hospitality" (Romans 12:13). The author of Hebrews says, "Do not neglect to show hospitality to strangers, for thereby some have entertained angels unawares" (Hebrews 13:2). And Jesus said that we would be judged by our hospitality, for when we love and welcome the needy, we love and welcome him (Matthew 25:35–40).

Strauch concludes, "Hardly anything is more characteristic of Christian love than hospitality. Through the ministry of hospitality we share the things we value most: family, home, financial resources, food, privacy, and time. In other words, we share our lives."[12]

SELF-EVALUATION

Because of our sinful tendency toward comfort, and because of the discomfort often associated with hospitality, we can all too easily avoid God's clear command. Engage with these questions and be honest with yourself and with God:

- *How many people from your church have you invited into your home for a meal? When was the last time someone stayed the night?*

- *Do others come to you when they need help, or do you give the impression that you don't want to be bothered?*

- *Is your family intentional about welcoming others into your home, even if they are different from you and make you feel awkward and uncomfortable? Do you only invite close friends into your home, or do you also welcome strangers?*

- *Why do you fear welcoming others into your life and your home? Which of God's promises can you cling to for hope, peace, and assurance?*

PRAYER POINTS

Take heart in the truth that the God of the weak and the outcast welcomes you—and ask him for help in these ways:

- *I pray that you would fill me with your Spirit so that my life bears fruit through good deeds that benefit others.*

- *I pray that I would hold loosely to all you have given me and know that my home, my food, my time, and everything else belong to you. Help me faithfully steward all of them.*

- *I pray that you would give me the compassion to welcome others as you have welcomed me.*

- *I pray that my motivation in hospitality would be to glorify you by showing others your perfect love. Please give me great joy and freedom in hospitality.*

CHAPTER 5

Gentle

As we continue our look at the character of the Christian—character that is to be present in every Christian and exemplified in pastors or elders—we turn to the wonderful and often overlooked trait of gentleness.

Paul writes to Timothy, "Therefore an overseer must be ... not violent but gentle, not quarrelsome" (1 Timothy 3:2–3). Similarly, he tells Titus that an overseer "must not be arrogant or quick-tempered ... or violent" (Titus 1:7). The positive characteristic here is gentleness, and it is opposed by the two negative characteristics of violence and quarreling. Following the elder's example, Christians must pursue gentleness and flee from violence and bickering.

To be gentle is to be tender, humble, and fair, to know what response is fitting for any occasion. It indicates graciousness, an extension of mercy, and a posture of submission to God's will and others' preferences. Such gentleness must be first expressed in the home and then subsequently in the church. Though it is a rare trait, we recognize and admire it in those who possess it.

Strauch notes that to pursue gentleness is to imitate Jesus. He writes,

> Jesus tells us who he is as a person: he is gentle and humble. Too many religious leaders, however, are not gentle nor are they humble. They are controlling and proud. They use people to satisfy their fat egos. But Jesus is refreshingly different. He truly loves people, selflessly serving and giving his life for them. He

expects his followers—especially the elders who lead his people—to be humble and gentle like himself."[13]

Similarly, John Piper writes, "This [gentleness] is the opposite of pugnacious or belligerent. He should not be harsh or mean-spirited. He should be inclined to tenderness and resort to toughness only when the circumstances commend this form of love. His words should not be acid or divisive but helpful and encouraging."[14]

The elder then must be "inclined to tenderness," able to control his response to others when he is attacked, maligned, or thrown into tense situations. He is marked at all times by patience, meekness, and a kind spirit. Negatively, he must not lose control either physically or verbally. He must control his temper, not responding to others with physical force or threats of violence. And he must control his tongue, not quarreling or bickering or asking for an argument. Even when pushed and exasperated, he will not lash out with his words. He will not crush a bruised reed or snuff out a faintly burning wick.

I am sure you realize that God calls all Christians—not just elders—to be gentle. Elders must serve as examples of gentleness, but each one of us must follow our elders, and ultimately our Savior, by displaying this trait. There are many texts we can turn to, like Galatians 5:22-23, which tells us that gentleness is a necessary fruit of the Spirit: "But the fruit of the Spirit is love, joy, peace, patience, kindness, goodness, faithfulness, gentleness, self-control." Shortly thereafter Paul says, "Brothers, if anyone is caught in any transgression, you who are spiritual should restore him in a spirit of gentleness" (Galatians 6:1).

He urges the Christians in Ephesus to "walk in a manner worthy of the calling to which you have been called," which involves living "with all humility and gentleness, with patience, bearing with one another in love, eager to maintain the unity of the Spirit in the bond of peace" (Ephesians 4:1–3). In another letter, Paul tells Titus to remind the congregation in Crete "to be submissive to rulers and authorities, to be obedient, to be ready for every good work, to speak evil of no one, to avoid quarreling, to be gentle, and to show perfect courtesy toward all people" (Titus 3:1–2). The evidence is clear: we are to be gentle so we can serve as a display of the one who deals so gently with us.

SELF-EVALUATION

Remember, as we study the character of a Christian, we must pause and reflect on whether we're applying these traits, lest we become only hearers of the Word. So, how are you doing in displaying gentleness? I encourage you to prayerfully ask yourself questions like these:

- *When someone wrongs you, are you prone to lash out in anger? If so, does that anger express itself physically, verbally, or both?*

- *Are people afraid to confront sin in your life because they fear your anger or your cutting words? Do your wife and children fear you in this way?*

- *Would your colleagues, friends, and family say that you are gentle? Would they say that you treat them with tenderness?*

- *Do you enjoy playing the devil's advocate? Do you like a good argument? What would your social media presence indicate?*

PRAYER POINTS

We can only obtain true gentleness by coming to the one who is "gentle and lowly in heart" (Matthew 11:29). So I encourage you to pray in these ways:

- *I pray that you would make me more like Christ, so that I may be gentle just as he is gentle. I pray that I would regularly consider all the ways you have been so patient and gentle with me.*

- *I pray that you would help me swallow my pride, confess my sins to others, and restore any strained relationships I have.*

- *I pray that you would give me the grace to be patient and calm when others attack and misunderstand me. Help me respond with gentleness even in the most difficult circumstances.*

- *I pray that I would be slow to begin an argument or wade into someone else's.*

CHAPTER 6

Temperate

We now have to explore what it means for Christian leaders and for all Christians to be temperate and sober rather than drunk or debauched.

Paul tells Timothy, "An overseer must be ... not a drunkard (1 Timothy 3:2–3). Again, he tells Titus that elders cannot be "open to the charge of debauchery" or "a drunkard" (Titus 1:5–7). Why this specific qualification? What is so important about it?

Strauch says plainly, "Drunkenness is sin, and persistently drunken people require church discipline.... So a person in a position of trust and authority over other people can't have a drinking problem."[15] Again, he writes, "If an elder has a drinking problem, he will lead people astray and bring reproach upon the church. His overindulgence will interfere with spiritual growth and service, and it may well lead to more degrading sins." It is worth noting that the Bible does not lay the blame for drunkenness on alcohol itself, but on the one consuming it. Commenting on 1 Timothy 3, John Stott points out that Paul "did not require them to be total abstainers, since Jesus himself changed water into wine and made wine the emblem of his blood.... What Paul requires, however, is moderation, as an example of the self-mastery already mentioned."[16]

John Piper widens the passage's implications when he says, "The general qualification here would be like the one above under temperance, namely, self-control—not addicted to anything harmful or debilitating or worldly. Freedom from enslavements should be so highly prized that no bondage is yielded to."[17] Piper extends the reach of this command from alcohol to any other kind of intoxicant or narcotic—a common and, I believe, fair extension of the principle.

As we have seen for each of these qualifications, God requires all Christians—not just elders—to pursue the same standards. Paul tells the church at Corinth that they must not associate or eat with "anyone who bears the name of brother" who is a "drunkard" (1 Corinthians 5:11). Why? Because along with other unrepentant sinners, drunkards "will not inherit the kingdom of God" (1 Corinthians 6:9–10). Again, Paul names drunkenness among the works of the flesh and says that "those who do such things will not inherit the kingdom of God" (Galatians 5:21). Elsewhere, he commands, "Do not get drunk with wine, for that is debauchery, but be filled with the Spirit" (Ephesians 5:18). Peter agrees: "The time that is past suffices for doing what the Gentiles want to do, living in sensuality, passions, drunkenness ..." (1 Peter 4:3).

The Proverbs also repeatedly warn against drunkenness. "Wine is a mocker, strong drink a brawler, and whoever is led astray by it is not wise" (Proverbs 20:1). "Be not among drunkards or among gluttonous eaters of meat" (Proverbs 23:20). Consider this passage:

> Who has woe? Who has sorrow? Who has strife? Who has complaining? Who has wounds without cause? Who has redness of eyes? Those who tarry long over wine; those who go to try mixed wine. Do not look at wine when it is red, when it sparkles in the cup and goes down smoothly. In the end it bites like a serpent and stings like an adder. Your eyes will see strange things, and your heart utter perverse things. You will be like one who lies down in the midst of the sea, like one who lies on the top of a mast. "They struck me," you will say, "but I was not hurt; they beat me, but I did not

feel it. When shall I awake? I must have another drink."
(Proverbs 23:29–35)

Finally, specific groups of people are also told to be sober. Deacons are held to the following standard: "Deacons likewise must be ... not addicted to much wine" (1 Timothy 3:8). And again Paul writes, "Older women likewise are to be ... not slaves to much wine" (Titus 2:3).

Regardless of your personal view on alcohol, this is certain: God's people are to be enslaved only to Jesus Christ (Romans 6:18). They are to resist any competitors, including alcohol.

SELF-EVALUATION

It is easy for us to hear the word of God and simply forget. As we read about moderation, we can begin to justify our habits and excuse our sin. To guard yourself from deceit and pursue the character of a Christian, I encourage you to ask yourself questions like these:

- *Do you have a biblically informed position on whether Christians may drink alcohol? Do you abide by your position? Do you stand in judgment against those who hold the opposite position?*

- *If your conscience permits you, are you able to drink alcohol in moderation, without becoming even slightly intoxicated? Would your friends and your family agree?*

- *Do you find yourself tempted to drink too close to your limit? Do you regularly succumb to the temptation to have "just one more drink"?*

- *Are there any other substances that you are addicted to? Do you look to these for the happiness and satisfaction that only Christ can provide?*

PRAYER POINTS

Whether you drink regularly, occasionally, or not at all, we all need God's help in maintaining moderation and pursuing holiness. To this end, I encourage you to pray like this:

- *I pray that you would deepen my convictions about alcohol so that I can partake (or abstain) with freedom and confidence. Help me never to violate my conscience, never unfairly pass judgment on others, and never flaunt my freedom.*

- *I pray that I would be able to enjoy your gifts without becoming enslaved to them. I pray that you would give me victory over all drunkenness and indulgence. I pray that you would help me never to relax my guard but always be vigilant.*

- *I pray that you would make me more like Christ, who was around alcohol and those who consumed it but never overindulged and always obeyed the Father.*

CHAPTER 7

Generous

This chapter will consider what it means for Christian leaders and for all Christians to reject the love of money and embrace love for others through generosity.

Paul tells Timothy, "An overseer must be … not a lover of money" (1 Timothy 3:2-3). Likewise, he tells Titus that an overseer "must not be … greedy for gain" (Titus 1:7). Finally, Peter writes to exiled elders, "Shepherd the flock of God … not for shameful gain, but eagerly" (1 Peter 5:2). Clearly, the biblical authors understand that the way we use our money displays something very important about our relationship with God. They also understand that there will always be those who use ministry for their own enrichment.

Ryken points out that there are two common errors when considering how Christian leaders relate to money:

> It is a grave mistake to consider wealth a credential for spiritual leadership. Being rich does not disqualify a man from the eldership, but it does not recommend him for it, either. What matters is how he uses his money, and especially how much affection he has for it. An overseer must not be a money-lover.[18]

Thus, John Piper writes that an elder's "lifestyle should not reflect a love of luxury. He should be a generous giver. He should not be anxious about his financial future. He should not be so money-oriented that ministry decisions revolve around this issue."[19] The man should be free from both the love of money and the love of the lavish lifestyle that money can buy. He displays his freedom from the love of money through his generosity.

Strauch explains,

This qualification prohibits a base, mercenary interest that uses Christian ministry and people for personal profit.... Like a powerful drug, the love of money can delude the judgment of even the best men.... Elders, then, cannot be the kind of men who are always interested in money. They cannot be men who need to control the church's funds and who refuse financial accountability. Such men have distorted spiritual values and set the wrong example for the church. They will inevitably fall into unethical financial dealings that will publicly disgrace the Lord's name.[20]

And indeed, we regularly see men fall into scandal for that very reason. Jesus warned, "You cannot serve God and money," since you can have only one master (Matthew 6:24). It is crucial to the well-being of the church that its leaders are joyfully controlled by the Word of God rather than the desire for wealth.

How about Christians who are not elders? Not surprisingly, God requires the very same standard. Jesus warned, "Do not lay up for yourselves treasures on earth, where moth and rust destroy and where thieves break in and steal, but lay up for yourselves treasures in heaven, where neither moth nor rust destroys and where thieves do not break in and steal. For where your treasure is, there your heart will be also" (Matthew 6:19–21). In Paul's letter to Timothy, he warns about the power of money: "Those who desire to be rich fall into temptation, into a snare, into many senseless and harmful desires that plunge people into ruin and destruction. For the love of money is a root of all kinds of evils. It is through this craving that some have wandered away from the faith and pierced themselves with many pangs" (1 Timothy 6:7–10). The Old Testament also contains several warnings like these. For example, one of the major themes of the Bible's wisdom literature is the danger of idolizing money and wealth.

It would be a great mistake, however, to think that God only has negative things to say about money. Rather, he tells us that money is a great gift that we can faithfully steward for the most significant purposes. "Honor the LORD with your wealth and with the first fruits of all your produce," says Solomon (Proverbs 3:9). When David was collecting offerings for the construction of the temple, "The people rejoiced because they had given willingly, for with a whole heart they had offered freely to the LORD" (1 Chronicles 29:9). Paul teaches the enduring value of generosity when he writes to the church in Corinth: "Each one must give as he has decided in his heart, not reluctantly or under compulsion, for God loves a cheerful giver" (2 Corinthians 9:7).

It is the Christian's duty and delight to hold loosely to wealth and give generously to the Lord's work. The problem of money is not with money itself, but with the self-serving bent of the human heart. But as Thabiti Anyabwile points out, Christians can be captivated by something so much greater than money: "The Lord gives us greater loves than money, which makes wings and flies away (Proverbs 23:5). He gives us greater delights in Christ, who in fact is the greatest delight of all. What a privilege it is, by God's rich grace, to preach Christ the Lamb to a world overrun with love for money."[21]

SELF-EVALUATION

Reading about God's call for generosity can either make us loosen our grip on money out of love for Jesus or tighten our grip on money out of fear of losing luxury. We need to examine ourselves to determine whether God or money is truly our master. I encourage you to prayerfully reflect on questions like these:

- *Would others say that you are stingy or generous? Would they say that you love money or that you love people?*

- *When was the last time you denied yourself a material pleasure so that you might use that money to bless someone else?*

- *Do you have a plan for your giving to the church and other worthy causes?*

- *Do you give secretly so that no one knows about it except for you and God, or do you give in order to be seen by others (Matthew 6:1–4)?*

PRAYER POINTS

God loves a cheerful giver because he himself is a cheerful giver. To become more like our generous Father, I encourage you to pray in these ways:

- *I pray that you, Father, would make Christ more precious to me than anything else—including money.*

- *I pray that you would give me a generous heart that is quick to identify and meet the needs of others. Help me to gladly lay up treasures in heaven with greater enthusiasm than I lay up treasures here on earth (Matthew 6:19–24).*

- *I pray that you would help me trust in you at all times—especially when finances are tight. Help me to believe that if you care for the birds of the air and clothe the grass of the field, then you will surely provide for me as well (Matthew 6:25–34).*

- *I pray that I would worship you as I willingly and generously give to your work each Sunday.*

CHAPTER 8

Family Leaders

This chapter will address why it's important for parents—both elders and all Christians—to lead their families in a God-honoring way.

We read in 1 Timothy 3:4–5, "[An elder] must manage his own household well, with all dignity keeping his children submissive, for if someone does not know how to manage his own household, how will he care for God's church?" Paul likewise tells Titus that an elder is qualified if his "children are believers and not open to the charge of debauchery or insubordination" (Titus 1:5–6). So what does that mean, and why is it so important?

Quite simply, it means that a man's leadership within the home proves his ability to lead within the church. Conversely, an inability to lead within the home proves an inability to lead within the church. In this way, the home rather than the office or classroom is the testing ground of a man's leadership ability. Why? As Strauch explains:

> Managing the local church is more like managing a family than managing a business or state. A man may be a successful businessman, a capable public official, a brilliant office manager, or a top military leader but be a terrible church elder or father. Thus a man's ability to oversee his household well is a prerequisite for overseeing God's household.[22]

Then what does it mean for a man to manage his household well? John Piper explains, "He should have submissive children. This does not mean perfect, but it does mean well-disciplined, so that they do not blatantly and regularly disregard the instructions of their parents. The children should revere the father. He should be a loving and responsible spiritual leader in the home."[23]

Again, if a man cannot tenderly lead and sacrificially love his own family, he must not be given the privilege and responsibility of leadership in the church. If he cannot excel at the one, he will not excel at the other. Thus if a man has a family, any process of evaluating him as a candidate for eldership must involve a close look within his home. Thabiti Anyabwile warns of "men who could be too preoccupied with the affairs of the church and too little occupied with what's going on under their own roof. One thinks of Eli's hasty and mistaken rebuke of Hannah as she prayed, while simultaneously abdicating responsibility for his wayward boys (1 Samuel 1–2). An elder tends to affairs at home."[24]

And what about the requirement that the elder's "children are believers"? This is a tricky text that has been the subject of much discussion, but I find myself in substantial agreement with Justin Taylor's skillful handling of the passage. He points out that the word translated as "believers" can also be translated as "faithful." This translation allows the text to nicely complement 1 Timothy 3:4 with its emphasis on control, obedience, and submission. He concludes, "What must not characterize the children of an elder is immorality and undisciplined rebelliousness, if the children are still at home and under his authority."[25]

Now, what about Christian parents who are not elders? How do we honor the text even as we widen its application? The answer is that all Christian parents must exhibit skill and godliness in their family relationships. Like the elders, they must seek to be exemplary. Fathers must lovingly lead and teach their children, not provoking them to anger, but bringing them up in the discipline of the Lord (Ephesians 6:4). Mothers must care for their children with love, managing their households with self-control and kindness" (Titus 2:3-5; 1 Timothy 5:14). Both father and mother are under God's charge toward Israel: "And these words that I command you today shall be on your heart. You shall teach them diligently to your children" (Deuteronomy 6:6–7).

Similarly, the Proverbs repeatedly portray the importance of disciplining your children. "Whoever spares the rod hates his son, but he who loves him is diligent to discipline him" (Proverbs 13:24). A host of narrative passages display the danger of neglecting such care and discipline. The author of Hebrews assumes the necessity of disciplining your children as an expression of your love for them. He asks, "What son is there whom his father does not discipline?" (Hebrews 12:7). His aim is to encourage Christians who are under the loving hand of God, who "disciplines us for our good, that we may share his holiness" (Hebrews 12:10).

From beginning to end, the Bible places upon every parent the responsibility to teach and train their children with kind, caring, and loving oversight.

SELF-EVALUATION

There is hope for the parent who has failed to lead their family well. But before you can pursue God's standard by his grace, you must recognize your shortcomings and turn from any area of sin. I challenge you to reflect on these questions below to see how you can grow in your leadership at home:

- *Do you look for ways to improve how you teach and discipline your family?*

- *When your family is in public, are your children out of control, or do they generally follow your lead and respond to your correction?*

- *Can you speak to your children's spiritual state? Do you know the condition of their souls? Do you pray for them in specific ways?*

- *Fathers, do you lead your family spiritually? Are family devotions part of your routine? Mothers, do you teach and train your children, do you pray with them, do you lovingly discipline them?*

PRAYER POINTS

Our heavenly Father is eager to help his children who are earthly fathers and mothers. Consider praying in these ways as you seek to humbly and boldly lead your family well:

- *I pray that you would make me a faithful and patient leader in my home.*

- *I pray that you would help me give both tough and tender love to my children.*

- *I pray that I would display the gospel in the way I love, lead, and care for my children.*

- *I pray that I would have a deeper understanding of God as Father, so that I can imitate him in the way I care for my children.*

CHAPTER 9

Mature and Humble

Here we will consider why elders and all Christians must strive to live mature and humble lives.

Paul tells Timothy, "[An elder] must not be a recent convert, or he may become puffed up with conceit and fall into the condemnation of the devil" (1 Timothy 3:6). In this call to spiritual maturity, we learn that elders must be mature for at least two reasons: because maturity begets humility and because immaturity begets pride and condemnation. Thus we must give positions of responsibility only to those who are spiritually mature. John Piper writes, "The new believer, given too much responsibility too soon, may easily swell with pride. The implication is that part of Christian seasoning is a humbling process and a growing protection against pride. We should see evidences in his life that humility is a fixed virtue and not easily overturned." [26]

Alexander Strauch says,

Maturity requires time and experience for which there is no substitute, so a new convert is simply not ready for the arduous task of shepherding God's flock. There is nothing wrong with being "a new convert." All Christians begin life in Christ as babies and grow to maturity. An elder, however, must be mature and know his own heart. A new Christian does not know his own heart or understand the craftiness of the enemy, so he is vulnerable to pride—the most subtle of all temptations and most destructive of all sins.

Again, he states, "If the elders are humble, the people will be humble, avoiding much contention. If the elders are servant leaders, the church will be marked by Christlike, humble servanthood."[27] God calls all Christians to maturity and humility—and such growth best takes place in the context of mature, humble leadership.

This call to maturity is given throughout God's Word, both to leaders and to all Christians. What elders are to model, all Christians are to possess. The author of the letter to the Hebrews says, "But solid food is for the mature, for those who have their powers of discernment trained by constant practice to distinguish good from evil" (Hebrews 5:14). He calls on this congregation to "leave the elementary doctrine of Christ and go on to maturity" (Hebrews 6:1).

Likewise, Paul says that God gives pastors and teachers to the church "to equip the saints for the work of ministry, for building up the body of Christ, until we all attain to the unity of the faith and of the knowledge of the Son of God, to mature manhood, to the measure of the stature of the fullness of Christ" (Ephesians 4:12–13). He commends Epaphras for "always struggling on your behalf in his prayers, that you may stand mature and fully assured in all the will of God" (Colossians 4:12). God expects that his children will grow in maturity and that this will in turn lead to humility.

Therefore, in a sense, this topic of maturity and humility gets to the heart of this entire booklet: *The Character of the Christian*. All Christians are to follow their leaders' example by striving to become more like Christ and growing in spiritual maturity. As they grow in maturity, they will necessarily grow in humility.

SELF-EVALUATION

Part of spiritual maturity is having the humility and the hunger for righteousness to inspect yourself. By asking questions like the ones below, we can take one step farther away from immaturity and toward the upward call of God.

- *Are there evidences in your life that you are growing "in the grace and knowledge of our Lord and Savior Jesus Christ" (2 Peter 3:18)?*

- *Are you more spiritually mature now than you were one year ago? Two years ago? How would you know?*

- *Do you seek the credit and the glory of man, or are you happy with being unknown, so long as you have God's approval? Many Christians want to be thought of as servants, but not treated as servants. Is that you?*

- *In what ways would your parents, children, spouse, boss, and pastors say you need to grow?*

PRAYER POINTS

The faithfulness of God will hold us fast, even when our growth feels slow. Take heart as you pray in these ways:

- *I pray, Father, that you would make me more like your Son in every area of my life.*

- *I pray that you would expose the blind spots in my life and give me the grace to turn from my sin.*

- *I pray that I would take full advantage of your means of grace, so that through them I can become more like Christ.*

- *I pray that you would help me pursue true greatness by becoming a servant of all.*

CHAPTER 10

Respected by Outsiders

Here in the final chapter we will tackle what it means for elders—and all Christians—to be well thought of by outsiders. And, of course, we will ask why it matters.

Paul instructs Timothy, "Moreover, [an elder] must be well thought of by outsiders, so that he may not fall into disgrace, into a snare of the devil" (1 Timothy 3:7). Paul has already said that an elder "must be above reproach" before everyone (1 Timothy 3:2), so being "well thought of by outsiders" zeroes in on one specific group: those who are outside the church. Yes, even a man's standing before the world counts as we evaluate his suitability for leadership.

On this point, John Piper writes, "What it seems to mean is that a Christian leader should at least meet the standards of the world for decency and respectability, for the standards of the church should be higher."[28] This matters, for as Paul has written elsewhere, the glory of God is at stake: "You who boast in the law dishonor God by breaking the law. For, as it is written, 'The name of God is blasphemed among the Gentiles because of you'" (Romans 2:23–24).

So why include a man's outside reputation as a requirement for eldership? Alexander Strauch addresses it practically: "Non-Christians may know more about the character and conduct of the prospective elder than the church. Quite often the prospective elder's non-Christian fellow workers or relatives actually have more daily contact with the church leader than do the people in church." He also says,

If a pastor-elder has a reputation among non-believers as a dishonest businessman, womanizer, or adulterer, the unbelieving community will take special note of his hypocrisy. Non-Christians will say, 'He acts that way, and he's a church elder!' They will ridicule and mock him. They will scoff at the people of God. They will talk about him and will generate plenty of sinister gossip. They will raise tough, embarrassing questions. He will be discredited as a Christian leader and suffer disgrace and insults. His influence for good will be ruined and he will endanger the church's evangelistic mission. The elder will certainly become a liability to the church, not a spiritual asset.[29]

The gospel itself is at stake in the consistency or hypocrisy of its leaders.

Now, what exactly is the "snare of the devil" that so concerns Paul? I think John Stott gets to the heart of it when he says, "In his malicious eagerness to discredit the gospel, the devil does his best to discredit the ministers of the gospel."[30] If Satan can discredit the leaders before the watching world, he can discredit the church and its message. Strauch adds,

The devil is pictured as a cunning hunter (1 Peter 5:8). Using public criticism and the elder's own inconsistencies, the devil will entrap the unwary Christian into more serious sin—uncontrolled bitterness, angry retaliation, lying, further hypocrisy, and stubbornness of heart. What may begin as a small offense can become something far more destructive and evil. Therefore, an elder must have a good reputation with those outside the Christian community.[31]

What about Christians who are not elders? They also must pursue the respect of outsiders. For instance, Paul writes, "Walk in wisdom toward outsiders, making the best use of the time. Let your speech always be gracious, seasoned with salt, so that you may know how you ought to answer each person" (Colossians 4:5–6). Again, he states, "We urge you, brothers ... to aspire to live quietly, and to mind your own affairs, and to work with your hands, as we instructed you, so that you may walk properly before outsiders and be dependent on no one" (1 Thessalonians 4:10–12). Christians will "shine as lights in the world" when they live "without blemish in the midst of a crooked and twisted generation" (Philippians 2:15).

Similarly, Peter commands, "Keep your conduct among the Gentiles honorable, so that when they speak against you as evildoers, they may see your good deeds and glorify God on the day of visitation.... For this is the will of God, that by doing good you should put to silence the ignorance of foolish people" (1 Peter 2:12, 15; see also 1 Peter 3:13–17). What is to be modeled by the church's leaders is to be obvious in every life. You, too, bear the responsibility to live an unblemished life before the world.

SELF-EVALUATION

Christians rightly tend to consider what God thinks about them and what fellow Christians think about them. But in light of the charge to be well thought of by outsiders, we also do well to consider what outsiders think about us, whether we are matching and outdoing the world's standards of decency and respectability.

- *Do you know your neighbors? Do they know you well*

enough to be able to speak to your character and reputation? How would your unbelieving neighbors describe you and your family?

- *What kind of reputation do you have among the unbelievers you work with? Do you work hard and avoid meddling (1 Thessalonians 4:10–12; Ephesians 4:28)?*

- *What would your unbelieving family members say is most important to you? Would they say that your life matches your profession?*

PRAYER POINTS

God is able to make more grace abound in your life, so I encourage you to join me in praying these ways:

- *I pray that you would make my life reflect the fruit of the Spirit so that my life would glorify, not shame, your name (Galatians 5:22-23).*

- *I pray that you would help me think about how my attitudes and actions affect others—especially unbelievers.*

- *I pray that I would model hard work and respect for authority, and that I would mind my own business in the workplace.*

- *I pray that I would be a model of good works at home, at work, and in my neighborhood, so that by doing good to others you would be glorified.*

Thanks for joining me through this booklet. I believe that God has helped me grow in the grace and knowledge of our Lord Jesus Christ as I've explored and applied his Word. I hope you can say the same! May God help you and help me to live an exemplary life that displays the character of the Christian.

NOTES

1   D.A. Carson, https://www.youtube.com/watch?v=mwA6_zDm2d8

2   There are three primary texts discussing the qualifications of an elder: 1 Timothy 3:2–7, Titus 1:6–9, and 1 Peter 5:1–3. Each of these overlaps with the others but each also has unique elements. We come to the fullest understanding of the elders' qualifications when we hold the three of them together. For the breakdown of the character qualities, I have followed the pattern Thabiti Anyabwile uses in *Finding Faithful Elders and Deacons*.

3   John MacArthur, *The Call to Lead the Church— Elders, Part 2.*

4   Alexander Strauch, *Biblical Eldership.*

5   John MacArthur, *The Call to Lead the Church— Elders, Part 4.*

6   Alexander Strauch, *Biblical Eldership.*

7   Philip Ryken, *1 Timothy: Reformed Expository Commentary.*

8   Thabiti Anyabwile, *Finding Faithful Elders and Deacons.*

9   Thabiti Anyabwile, *Finding Faithful Elders and Deacons.*

10 Alexander Strauch, *Biblical Eldership.*

11 Alexander Strauch, *Biblical Eldership.*

12 Alexander Strauch, *Biblical Eldership.*

13 Alexander Strauch, *Biblical Eldership.*

14 John Piper, *Biblical Eldership Session 1.*

15 Alexander Strauch, *Biblical Eldership.*

Notes

16 John Stott, *The Message of 1 Timothy & Titus: The Bible Speaks Today.*

17 John Piper, *Rethinking the Governance Structure at Bethlehem Baptist Church.*

18 Philip Ryken, *1 Timothy: Reformed Expository Commentary.*

19 John Piper, *Rethinking the Governance Structure at Bethlehem Baptist Church.*

20 Alexander Strauch, *Biblical Eldership.*

21 Thabiti Anyabwile, *Finding Faithful Elders and Deacons.*

22 Alexander Strauch, *Biblical Eldership.*

23 John Piper, *Rethinking the Governance Structure at Bethlehem Baptist Church.*

24 Thabiti Anyabwile, *Finding Faithful Elders and Deacons.*

25 Justin Taylor, *You Asked: Does an Unbelieving Child Disqualify an Elder?*

26 John Piper, *Rethinking the Governance Structure at Bethlehem Baptist Church.*

27 Alexander Strauch, *Biblical Eldership.*

28 John Piper, *Rethinking the Governance Structure at Bethlehem Baptist Church.*

29 Alexander Strauch, *Biblical Eldership.*

30 John Stott, *The Message of 1 Timothy & Titus: The Bible Speaks Today.*

31 Alexander Strauch, *Biblical Eldership.*

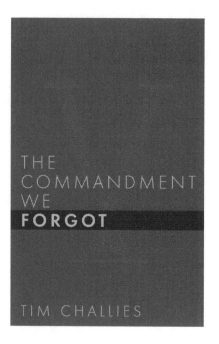

The Commandment We Forgot
Tim Challies

The fifth commandment— "Honor your father and your mother"— is not just for children. Rather, it pertains to the whole of life and to every person of every age. In the home, the church, and the workplace, it provides a stable foundation for all of society. Yet we often neglect it and fail to appreciate its relevance to our lives. It is the commandment we forgot.

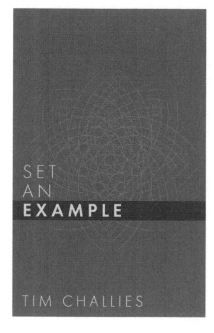

Set an Example
Tim Challies

There are many ways to invest your time in your teens and 20's, but the Bible is clear: none is better than the pursuit of godliness. In Paul's letter to young Timothy, you (yes, you!) are called to be an example to your peers and even to older Christians. He calls you to set an example of maturity and godliness in your speech, conduct, love, faith, and purity.